My Spelling Workbook

This book belongs to:

....

My Spelling Workbook *(Book A)*

Published by Prim-Ed Publishing 2011
3rd edition 2021
Reprinted 2015, 2021, 2022, 2023, 2025
Copyright© Prim-Ed Publishing 2011
ISBN 978-1-80087-108-3
PR–2280

Titles available in this series:
My Spelling Workbook *(Book A)*
My Spelling Workbook *(Book B)*
My Spelling Workbook *(Book C)*
My Spelling Workbook *(Book D)*
My Spelling Workbook *(Book E)*
My Spelling Workbook *(Book F)*
My Spelling Workbook *(Book G)*

Copyright Notice
No part of this book may be reproduced in any form or by any means, electronic or mechanical, including photocopying or recording, or by an information retrieval system without written permission from the publisher.

Offices in:
UK and Republic of Ireland:
Unit 2A, Block E
Waterford Road Business Park
New Ross, Co. Wexford
Y34 NC82, Ireland
www.prim-ed.com

Australia:
PO Box 332, Greenwood
Western Australia 6924
www.ricpublications.com.au

Disclaimer
Every effort has been made to ensure quality of content and accuracy of information; our team at R.I.C. Publications® and Prim-Ed Publishing cannot be held responsible for mistakes or omissions, but we do endeavour to rectify any errors found within our products. Please contact us to provide feedback.

Introduction

Welcome to **My Spelling Workbook**.

This book and interactive download have lots of activities to help you learn to spell.

You should follow this method when you are learning to spell each word.

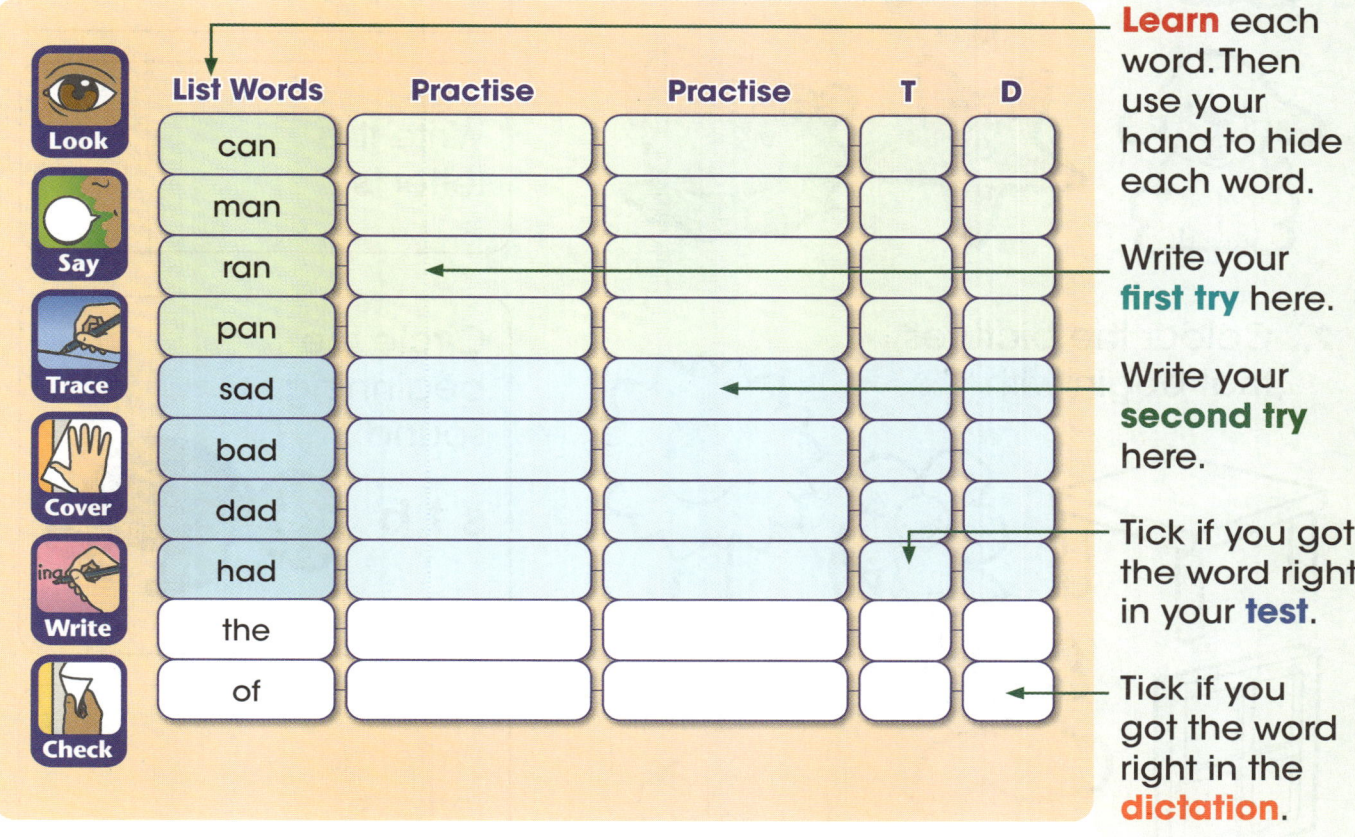

Contents

Beginning Sounds	2–13
Final Sounds	14–17
Medial Sounds	18–21
Unit 1 *an, ad*	22–23
Unit 2 *et, am*	24–25
Unit 3 *Christmas*	26–27
Unit 4 *in, ip*	28–29
Unit 5 *ot, it*	30–33
Unit 6 *ug, ag*	34–37
Unit 7 *ix, ox, ut*	38–41
Unit 8 *Long e, ed*	42–45
Unit 9 *Spring/Easter*	46–49
Unit 10 *eg, en*	50–53
Unit 11 *y, op*	54–57
Unit 12 *ee*	58–61
Unit 13 *oo, all*	62–65
Unit 14 *and, end*	66–69
Unit 15 *Summer Holidays*	70–73
Difficult Words I Have Found	74
My Spelling Dictionary Aa–Zz	75–78

My Spelling Workbook A—Prim-Ed Publishing—www.prim-ed.com

Beginning Sounds

1. Circle the pictures that begin with 's'.

2. Colour the pictures that begin with 't'.

3. Circle the pictures that begin with 'b'.

Circle the beginning sound.

s t b

Write the letter 's'.

Circle the beginning sound.

s t b

Write the letter 't'.

Circle the beginning sound.

s t b

Write the letter 'b'.

Beginning Sounds

4. Circle the pictures that begin with '**c**'.

Circle the beginning sound.

c f r

Write the letter '**c**'.

5. Colour the pictures that begin with '**f**'.

Circle the beginning sound.

c f r

Write the letter '**f**'.

6. Circle the pictures that begin with '**r**'.

Circle the beginning sound.

c f r

Write the letter '**r**'.

Beginning Sounds

1. Circle the pictures that begin with 'e'.

Circle the beginning sound.

e g h

Write the letter 'e'.

2. Colour the pictures that begin with 'g'.

Circle the beginning sound.

e g h

Write the letter 'g'.

3. Circle the pictures that begin with 'h'.

Circle the beginning sound.

e g h

Write the letter 'h'.

Beginning Sounds

4. Circle the pictures that begin with '**o**'.

Circle the beginning sound.

o m n

Write the letter '**o**'.

5. Colour the pictures that begin with '**m**'.

Circle the beginning sound.

o **m** n

Write the letter '**m**'.

6. Circle the pictures that begin with '**n**'.

Circle the beginning sound.

o m **n**

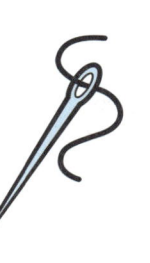

Write the letter '**n**'.

Beginning Sounds

1. Circle the pictures that begin with 'a'.

Circle the beginning sound.

a l w

Write the letter 'a'.

2. Colour the pictures that begin with 'l'.

Circle the beginning sound.

a l w

Write the letter 'l'.

3. Circle the pictures that begin with 'w'.

Circle the beginning sound.

a l w

Write the letter 'w'.

Beginning Sounds

4. Circle the pictures that begin with 'i'.

Circle the beginning sound.

i k p

Write the letter 'i'.

5. Colour the pictures that begin with 'k'.

Circle the beginning sound. i k p

Write the letter 'k'.

6. Circle the pictures that begin with 'p'.

Circle the beginning sound.

i k p

Write the letter 'p'.

Beginning Sounds

1. Circle the pictures that begin with '**d**'.

Circle the beginning sound.

d q u

Write the letter '**d**'.

2. Colour the pictures that begin with '**q**'.

Circle the beginning sound.

d q u

Write the letter '**q**'.

3. Circle the pictures that begin with '**u**'.

Circle the beginning sound.

d q u

Write the letter '**u**'.

Beginning Sounds

4. Colour the pictures that begin with '**j**'.

Circle the beginning sound.

j **v**

Write the letter '**j**'.

5. Circle the pictures that begin with '**v**'.

Circle the beginning sound.

j **v**

Write the letter '**v**'.

Beginning Sounds

1. Circle the picture that begins with 'x'.

Circle the beginning sound.

x y z

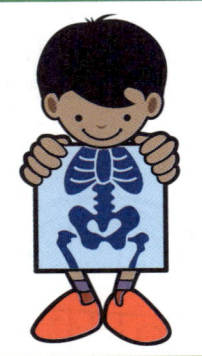

Write the letter 'x'.

2. Colour the pictures that begin with 'y'.

Circle the beginning sound.

x y z

Write the letter 'y'.

3. Circle the pictures that begin with 'z'.

Circle the beginning sound.

x y z

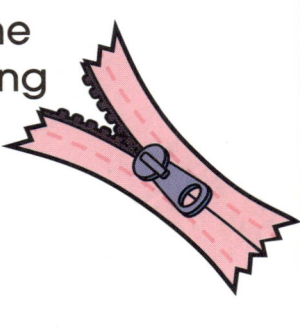

Write the letter 'z'.

Beginning Sounds

Circle the beginning sound.

Beginning Sounds

Write the beginning sound.

p o s x c d w a g t m b n f v

___og 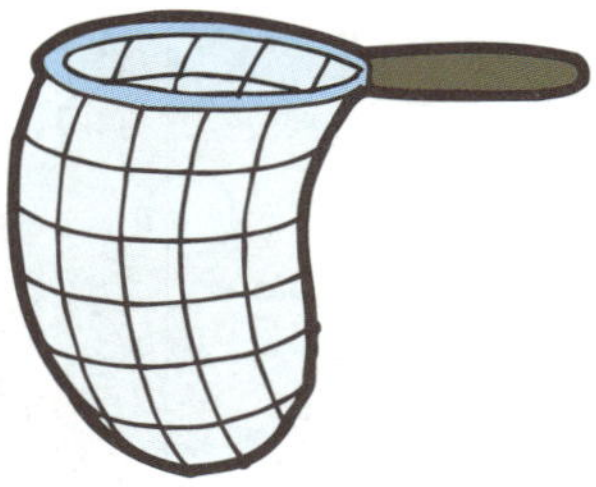   ___et 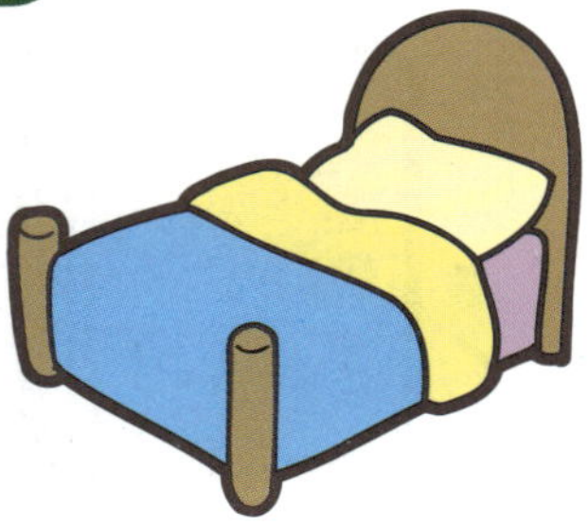   ___ed

___un    ___at    ___ate

___-ray    ___ap    ___nt

___ctopus    ___ig    ___ish

___eb    ___at    ___ase

Beginning Sounds

Write the beginning sound.

__et   __ip   __at

__oyo   __gg   __op

__est   __ox   __ug

__og   __ey   __nsect

__rum   __uack   __mbrella

e h l u i d q y j k n r z b m

Final Sounds

Circle the end sound.

Final Sounds

Circle the end sound.

Final Sounds

b m k t g d n p

Write the end sound.

ca___   ste___   bi___

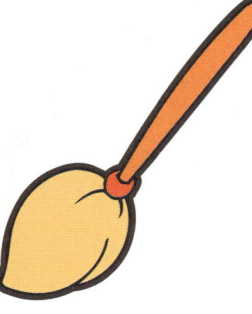

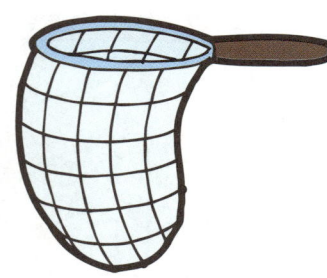

mo___   fro___   ne___

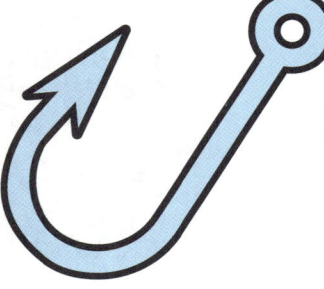

hoo___   li___   pi___

cu___   moo___   for___

Medial Sounds

1. (a) Circle the pictures with an 'a' sound in the middle.

(b) Circle the pictures with an 'i' sound in the middle.

2. Write 'a' or 'i' in the middle of each word.

p__g   b__t   f__n

b__n   f__n   m__p

Medial Sounds

1. (a) Circle the pictures with an 'e' sound in the middle.

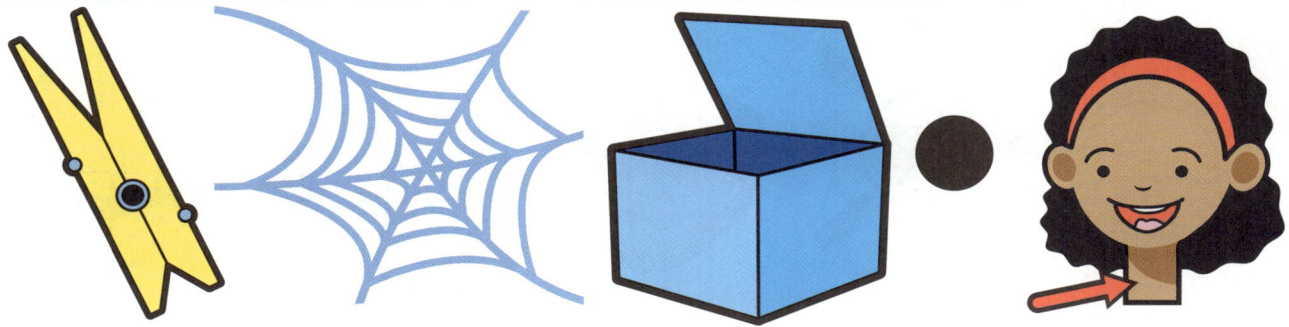

(b) Circle the pictures with an 'o' sound in the middle.

2. Write 'e' or 'o' in the middle of each word.

j__t   h__n   d__g

p__t   b__d   m__p

Medial Sounds

1. (a) Circle the pictures with an 'a' sound in the middle.

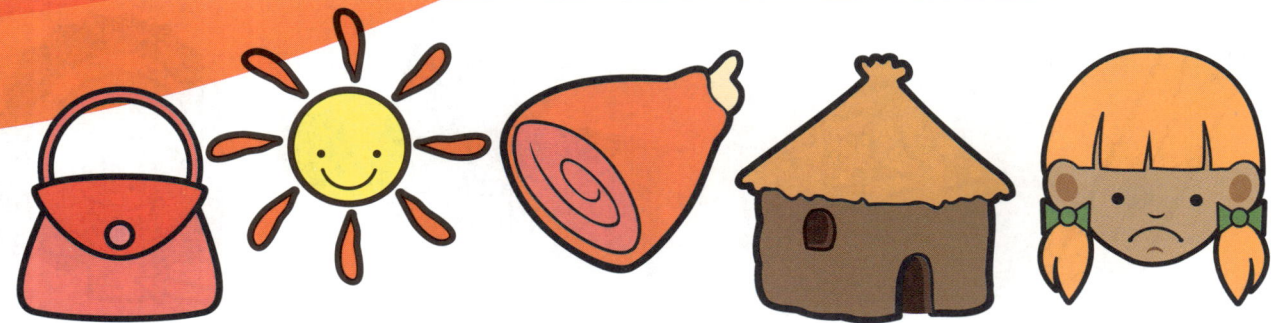

(b) Circle the pictures with an 'u' sound in the middle.

2. Write 'a' or 'u' in the middle of each word.

c__p   b__s   b__t

m__g   r__t   b__g

Medial Sounds

1. (a) Circle the pictures with an 'e' sound in the middle.

(b) Circle the pictures with an 'i' sound in the middle.

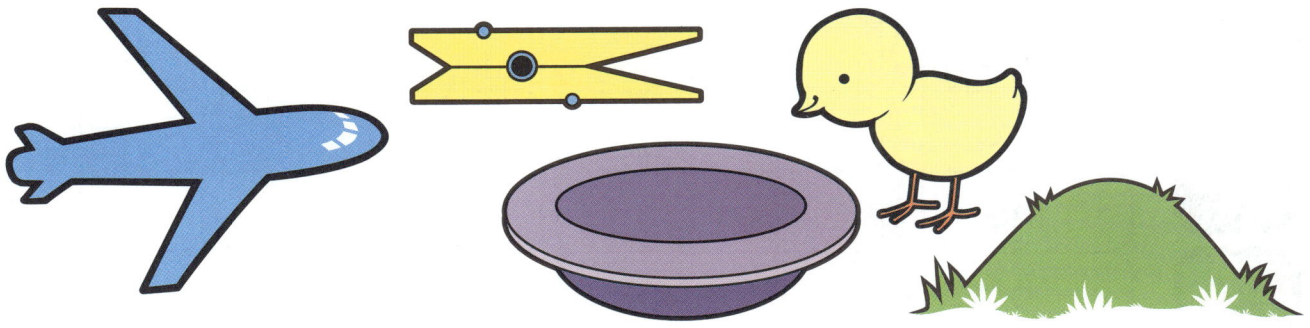

2. Write 'e' or 'i' in the middle of each word.

l__g   p__n   t__n

p__t   z__p   b__b

Unit 1

 Look
 Say
 Trace
 Cover
 Write
 Check

List Words	Practise	Practise	T	D
can				
man				
ran				
pan				
sad				
bad				
dad				
had				
the				
of				

Fill the Gaps

1. (a) can   (b) pan   (c) dad

   ca___   pa___   da___

   c___ ___   p___ ___   d___ ___

   ___ ___ ___ ___ ___ ___ ___ ___ ___

Word Worm

2. Circle each word you can find in the word worm.

   cansaddadrantheman

Unit 1

Spelling Sums

3. (a) c + an = __can__

   (b) r + an = _____

   (c) s + ad = _____

   (d) b + ad = _____

   (e) p + an = _____

Read and Draw

4. A sad man.

Shape Sorter

5. Guess the word by its shape.

   (a)
   (b)
   (c)
   (d)

Spelling Patterns

6. Use the correct colour for these words.

   (a) Colour the '**an**' words red.

   (b) Colour the '**ad**' words blue.

Unit 2

et am

List Words	Practise	Practise	T	D
pet				
met				
set				
wet				
am				
ham				
jam				
ram				
to				
by				

Look

Say

Trace

Cover

Write

Check

Fill the Gaps

1. (a) met (b) pet (c) ham

   me___   pe___   ha___

   m___ ___   p___ ___   h___ ___

   ___ ___ ___   ___ ___ ___   ___ ___ ___

Word Worm

2. Circle each word you can find in the word worm.

towetjambypetram

Unit 2

et am

Spelling Sums

3. (a) r + am = __ram__

   (b) w + et = _____

   (c) j + am = _____

   (d) h + am = _____

   (e) m + et = _____

Read and Draw

4. A jar of jam.

Shape Sorter

5. Guess the word by its shape.

(a)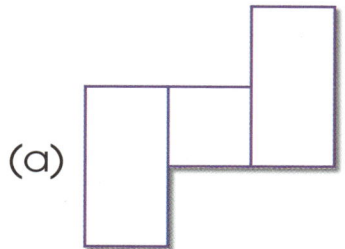

(b)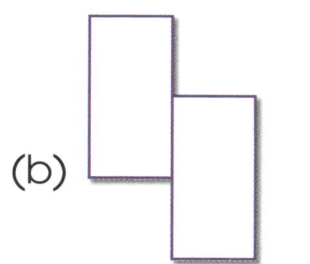

(c)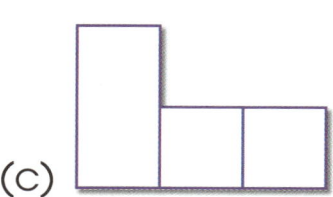

(d)

Spelling Patterns

6. Use the correct colour for these words.

   (a) Colour the 'et' words red.

   (b) Colour the 'am' words blue.

met   jam   ram

set   pet

ham

Unit 3 — Christmas

List Words	Practise	Practise	T	D
bells				
red				
star				
fun				
cake				
Santa				
tag				
tree				
did				
got				

Look · Say · Trace · Cover · Write · Check

Find the Word

1. Write each word on the grid.

   (a)
   (b)
   (c) You have it at the circus.
   (d)
   (e)

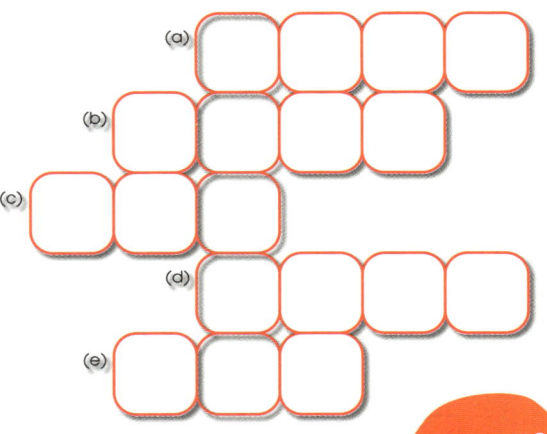

Word Worm

2. Circle each word you can find in the word worm.

redtagfuncakegotSanta

Christmas

Unit 3

Read and Draw

3. A Christmas tree.

Shape Sorter

5. Guess the word by its shape.

(a)

(b)

(c)

(d)

Word Search

4. Find these words in the word search.

bells   Santa
red   tag
star   tree
fun   did
cake
got

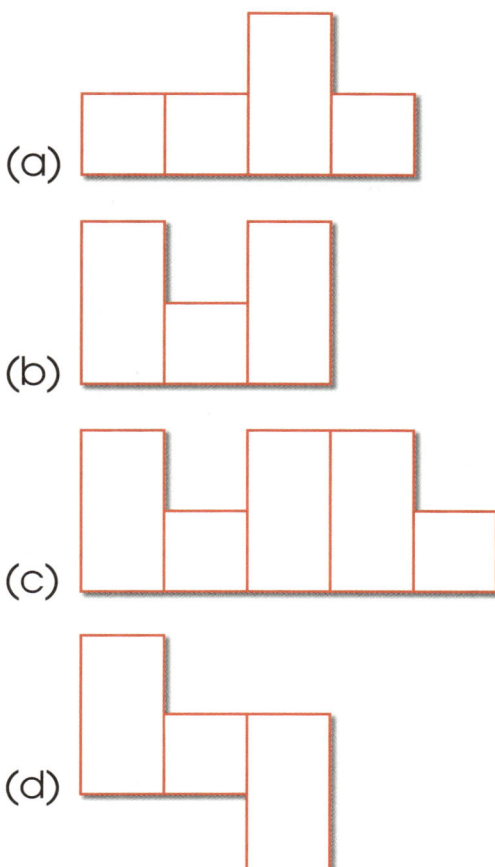

Rhyming Words

6. Write a Christmas word that rhymes with these words.

(a) bed _____

(b) bee _____

(c) sun _____

(d) car _____

(e) rag _____

(f) sells _____

Unit 4

List Words	Practise	Practise	T	D
win				
fin				
bin				
tin				
sip				
tip				
lip				
zip				
is				
you				

Fill the Gaps

1. (a) bin   (b) sip   (c) win

    bi___   si___   wi___

    b___ ___   s___ ___   w___ ___

    ___ ___ ___   ___ ___ ___   ___ ___ ___

Spelling Patterns

2. Use the correct colour for these words.

   (a) Colour the 'in' words red.

   (b) Colour the 'ip' words blue.

sip zip tip win fin tin

Unit 4

in　ip

Spelling Sums

3. (a) f + in = __fin__

   (b) b + in = _____

   (c) s + ip = _____

   (d) z + ip = _____

   (e) w + in = _____

Read and Draw

4. A tin of soup.

All Mixed Up

5. Unjumble these words.

   (a) pzi _____

   (b) uoy _____

   (c) nti _____

   (d) lpi _____

Word Worm

6. Circle each word you can find in the word worm.

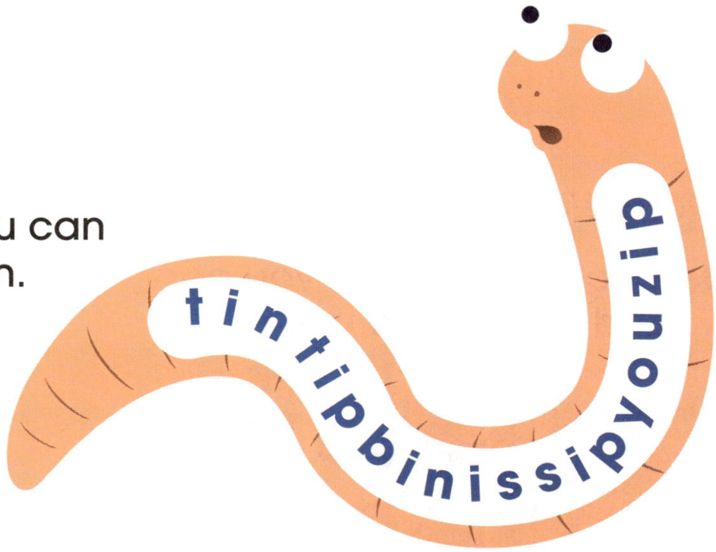

tintipbinissipyouzip

Unit 5

 Look
 Say
 Trace
 Cover
 Write
 Check

List Words	Practise	Practise	T	D
cot				
hot				
dot				
pot				
bit				
pit				
sit				
it				
that				
if				

Fill the Gaps

1. (a) dot (b) pit (c) cot

    do___   pi___   co___

    d___ ___   p___ ___   c___ ___

    ___ ___ ___   ___ ___ ___   ___ ___ ___

Word Worm

2. Circle each word you can find in the word worm.

ifhotpotthatbitdot

ot it

All Mixed Up

3. Unjumble these words.

   (a) fi _____

   (b) tsi _____

   (c) pto _____

   (d) ttha _____

Read and Draw

4. A hot sun.

Spelling Sums

5. (a) h + ot = __hot__

   (b) b + it = _____

   (c) p + ot = _____

   (d) c + ot = _____

   (e) s + it = _____

Spelling Patterns

6. Use the correct colour for these words.

   (a) Colour the 'ot' words green.

   (b) Colour the 'it' words red.

Unit 5

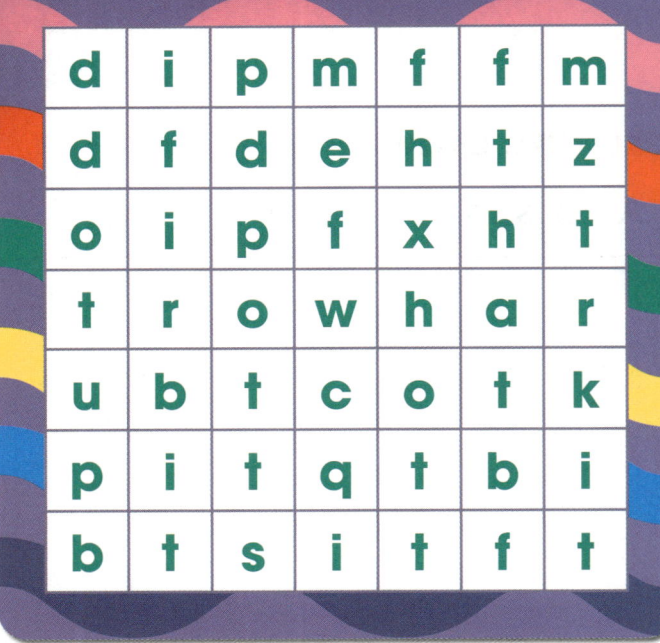

Word Search

7. Find these list words in the word search.

   hot   it   if   that   pot
   dot   pit   sit   bit   cot

Missing Letters

8. Write '**ot**' or '**it**' to make a word.

   (a) b___   (b) s___

   (c) c___   (d) d___

Missing Words

9. Complete the sentences using these words.

(a) It was so _____ today we went for a swim.

(b) Can I have a _____ of cake, please?

(c) _____ you go too fast, you will crash.

List Words

cot
hot
dot
pot
bit
pit
sit
it
that
if

Word Maker

10. How many words can you make?

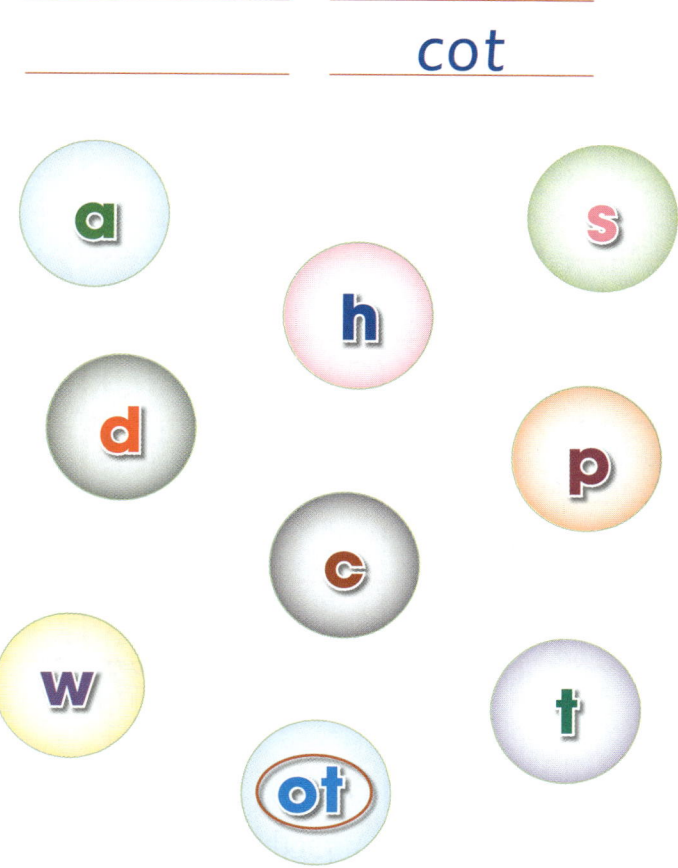

_____   _____

cot

What am I?

11. I am tiny.

I am round.

I am black.

I am a _____.

Draw Me

Match Me

12. Circle the word in the box that matches the given word.

(a) that — tat   that   tath   taht

(b) pit — pet   tip   pit   pot

(c) dot — dut   tod   top   dot

Unit 6

List Words	Practise	Practise	T	D
hug				
rug				
bug				
mug				
jug				
bag				
rag				
wag				
put				
was				

Fill the Gaps

1. (a) rug   (b) bag   (c) put

   ru___   ba___   pu___

   r_____   b_____   p_____

   _____   _____   _____

Spelling Patterns

2. Use the correct colour for these words.

   (a) Colour the 'ag' words dark green.

   (b) Colour the 'ug' words red.

Unit 6

ug ag

Spelling Sums

3. (a) j + ug = _jug_

   (b) b + ag = _____

   (c) m + ug = _____

   (d) b + ug = _____

   (e) w + ag = _____

Read and Draw

4. A jug of water.

All Mixed Up

5. Unjumble these words.

   (a) wga _____

   (b) tup _____

   (c) swa _____

   (d) gru _____

Word Worm

6. Circle each word you can find in the word worm.

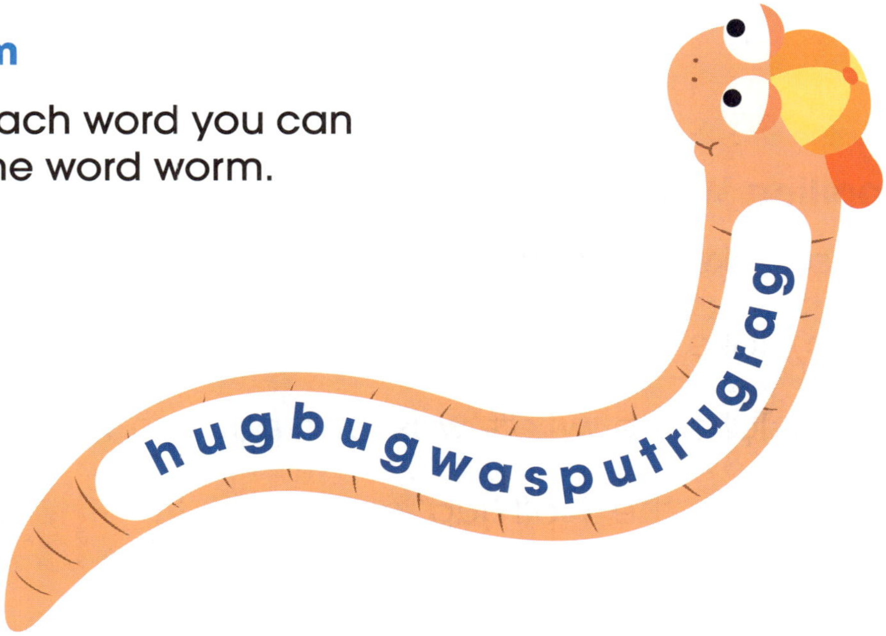

   hugbugwasputrugrag

Unit 6

b	j	z	j	m	h	e
u	w	a	g	u	u	p
g	d	j	z	g	g	u
s	r	u	b	c	c	t
b	a	g	q	r	k	w
y	f	a	v	u	l	a
g	t	r	a	g	u	s

Word Search

7. Find these words in the word search.

   hug   bag
   bug   rag
   rug   wag
   mug   put
   jug   was

More than One

8. Add 's' to make more than one.

   (a) mug _____   (b) bag _____
   (c) hug _____   (d) bug _____

Spelling Words

9. (a) Take the 'p' off 'put' and put in 'c'. _____
   (b) Take the 'u' off 'bug' and put in 'i'. _____
   (c) Take the 'w' off 'was' and put in 'h'. _____
   (d) Take the 'j' off 'jug' and put in 't'. _____

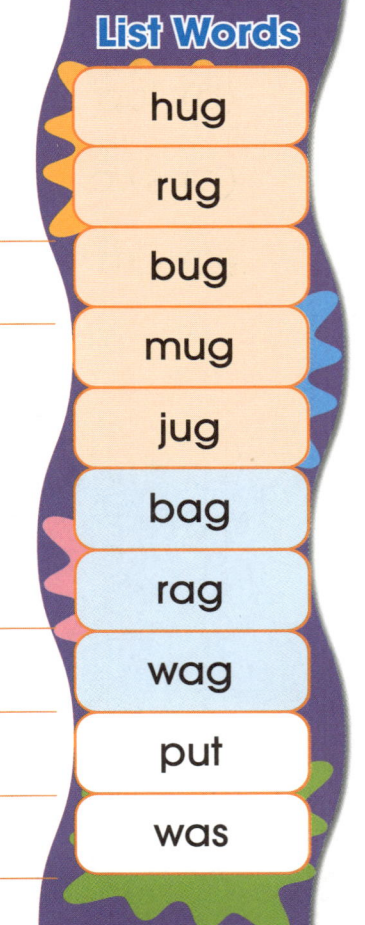

List Words: hug, rug, bug, mug, jug, bag, rag, wag, put, was

Unit 6

ug **ag**

Find Me

10. Circle the correct word.

(a) hug

jug

bug

(b) rug

mug

hug

(c) hug

mug

jug

(d) rag

wag

bag

Missing Letters

11. Write the missing letters.

(a) p___t

(b) m___ ___

(c) j___ ___

(d) w___s

(e) h___ ___

(e) wag

rag

bag

Word Hunt

12. (a) Which words start with 'w'? _____ _____

(b) Which word is often given by Mum or Dad? _____

(c) Which word is an insect? _____

Unit 7

Look

Say

Trace

Cover

Write

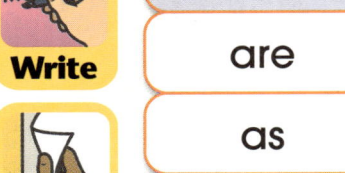
Check

List Words	Practise	Practise	T	D
mix				
six				
box				
fox				
cut				
hut				
but				
nut				
are				
as				

Fill the Gaps

1. (a) fox   (b) six   (c) nut

     fo___   si___   nu___

     f___ ___   s___ ___   n___ ___

     ___ ___ ___   ___ ___ ___   ___ ___ ___

Spelling Patterns

2. Use the correct colour for these words.

     (a) Colour the 'ix' and 'ox' words green.

     (b) Colour the 'ut' words red.

Unit 7

ix ox ut

Spelling Sums

3. (a) m + ix = __mix__

   (b) f + ox = _____

   (c) h + ut = _____

   (d) s + ix = _____

   (e) c + ut = _____

Read and Draw

4. A garden hut.

All Mixed Up

5. Unjumble these words.

   (a) tun _____

   (b) sa _____

   (c) rea _____

   (d) xbo _____

Word Worm

6. Circle each word you can find in the word worm.

cutsixaremixbox

Unit 7

Word Search

7. Find these words in the word search.

mix	hut
six	but
box	nut
fox	are
cut	as

What Am I?

8. I am hard and small.

   You can eat me.

   I am part of a fruit.

   I am a _____.

Missing Words

9. Complete the sentences using these words.

         fox

(a) He is _____ fast _____ the wind.

(b) An ant has _____ legs.

(c) A _____ has a big tail.

(d) We _____ going to school.

List Words: mix, six, box, fox, cut, hut, but, nut, are, as

Find Me

10. Circle the correct word.

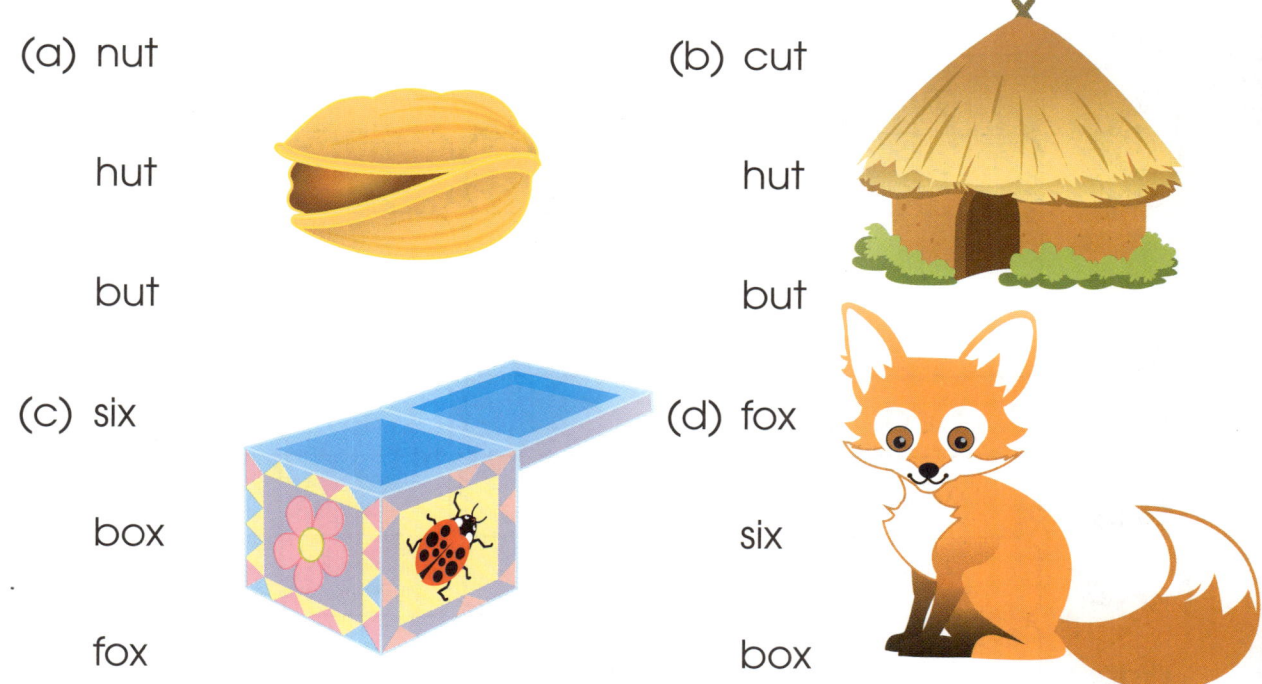

(a) nut
hut
but

(b) cut
hut
but

(c) six
box
fox

(d) fox
six
box

Match Me

11. Circle the word in the box that matches the given word.

(a) are — arr   are   ar

(b) but — but   bat   bet

(c) cut — cat   cute   cut

Secret Words

12. (a) Take the 'e' off 'are' and put in 't'. _____

(b) Take the 's' off 'as' and put in 't'. _____

(c) Take the 'u' off 'nut' and put in 'o'. _____

(d) Take the 'u' off 'but' and put in 'a'. _____

Unit 8

Long e | ed

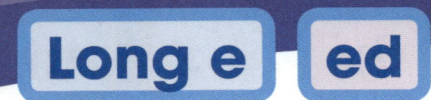

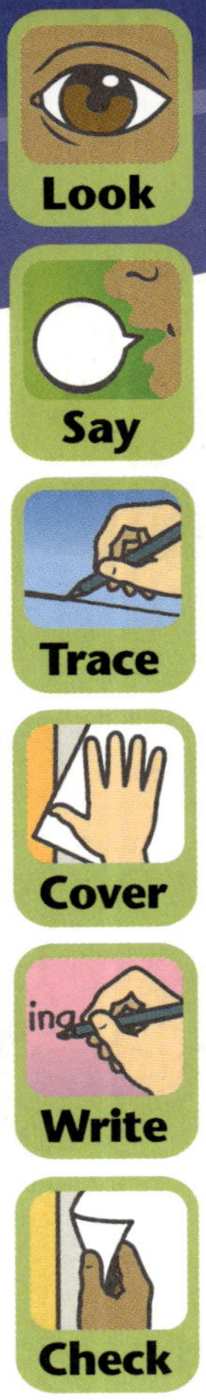

Look
Say
Trace
Cover
ing
Write
Check

List Words	Practise	Practise	T	D
we				
me				
he				
she				
be				
bed				
wed				
fed				
with				
his				

Fill the Gaps

1. (a) bed
be___
b___ ___
___ ___ ___

(b) she
sh___
s___ ___
___ ___ ___

(c) wed
we___
w___ ___
___ ___ ___

Spelling Patterns

2. Use the correct colour for these words.

(a) Colour the words ending in '**e**' orange.

(b) Colour the '**ed**' words green.

fed
wed
he
me
we
bed

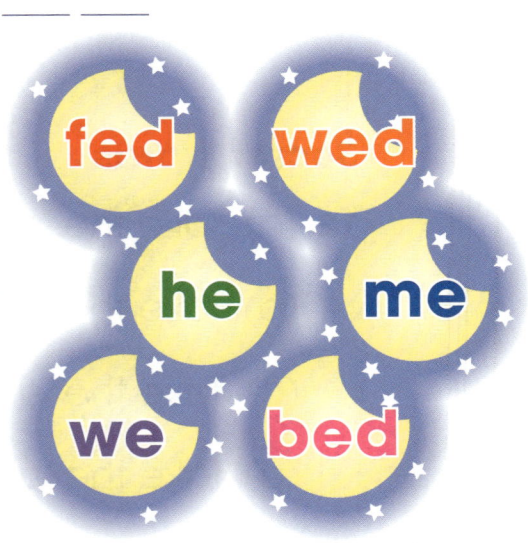

Long e ed

Unit 8

Spelling Sums

3. (a) b + ed = __bed__

   (b) wi + th = _____

   (c) f + ed = _____

   (d) w + ed = _____

   (e) sh + e = _____

Read and Draw

4. A boy with his teddy.

Word Worm

5. Circle each word you can find in the word worm.

Word Maker

6. How many words can you make?

   _____

   _____

   _____

Unit 8

Long e **ed**

v	h	b	e	d	o	n
h	i	c	g	b	e	f
y	s	r	r	s	h	e
z	s	w	l	w	h	d
i	f	e	z	i	m	m
b	r	d	p	t	h	e
w	e	s	f	h	i	z

Word Search

7. Find these words in the word search.

   we   bed

   me   wed

   he   fed

   she   with

   be   his

All Mixed Up

8. Unjumble these words.

   (a) def   _____

   (b) esh   _____

   (c) itwh   _____

   (d) deb   _____

Shape Sorter

9. Guess the word by its shape.

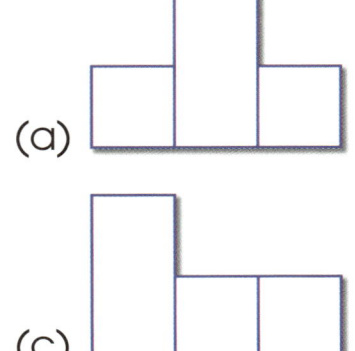

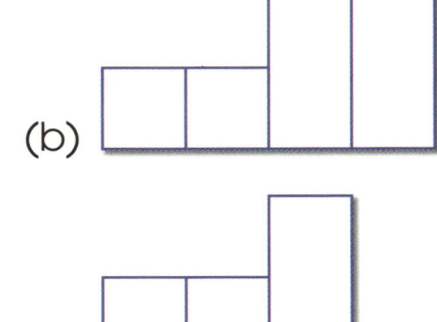

List Words: we, me, he, she, be, bed, wed, fed, with, his

Missing Words

10. Complete the sentences using these words.

be **She** **me** **with**

(a) _____ has pretty new shoes.

(b) Can you meet _____ tomorrow at the shops?

(c) I will _____ in bed by eight o'clock.

(d) Sam goes to bed _____ a teddy bear.

Match Me

11. Circle the word in the box that matches the given word.

(a) with — wif   wite   with

(b) bed — bead   bed   bad

(c) his — is   has   his

Word Hunt

12. (a) Which words have two letters? _____ _____ _____ _____

(b) Write the word that has 'th' in it. _____

(c) Which word has the small word 'he' in it? _____

Unit 9 — Spring/Easter

List Words	Practise	Practise	T	D
ant				
bee				
bud				
bug				
dig				
fog				
frog				
sun				
ask				
here				

Look · Say · Trace · Cover · Write · Check

Rhyming Words

1. Write a spring word that rhymes with these words.

   (a) hug _____   (b) mud _____

   (c) see _____   (d) bun _____

   (e) pant _____ (f) big _____

Find the Word

2. Write each word on the grid.

(a)

(b)

(c)

Spring/Easter

Unit 9

Read and Draw

3. A frog sitting in the sun.

All Mixed Up

4. Unjumble these words.

(a) gdi _____

(b) sak _____

(c) reeh _____

(d) dub _____

Shape Sorter

5. Guess the word by its shape.

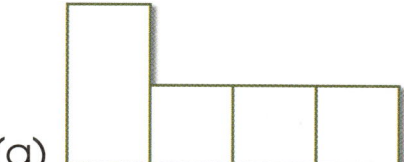

(a)

(b)

(c)

(d)

Word Worm

6. Circle each word you can find in the word worm.

digfogbeeaskhereant

Unit 9 — Spring/Easter

Word Search

7. Find these words in the Easter egg word search.

 ant   fog
 bee   frog
 bud   sun
 bug   ask
 dig   here

Missing Words

8. Complete the sentences using these words.

Dig   bee   Ask   fog

(a) _____ Mum if we can go out to play.

(b) It is hard to see in the _____.

(c) A _____ can buzz.

(d) _____ a hole for the new tree.

Word Maker

9. How many list words can you make from the letters on the Easter egg?

_____ _____ _____

48 My Spelling Workbook A—Prim-Ed Publishing—www.prim-ed.com

Spring/Easter

Unit 9

Labels

10. Label the pictures.

(a) _____

(b) _____

(c) _____

(d) _____

Word Hunt

11. (a) Which words start with 'b'?

_____ _____

_____

(b) Which words have four letters?

_____ _____

(c) Which word has the small word 'an' in it?

_____

Fill the Gaps

12. (a) here

her___

he___ ___

h___ ___ ___

___ ___ ___ ___

(b) ask

as___

a___ ___

___ ___ ___

(c) fog

fo___

f___ ___

___ ___ ___

List Words

- ant
- bee
- bud
- bug
- dig
- fog
- frog
- sun
- ask
- here

Unit 10

 Look
 Say
 Trace
 Cover
 Write
 Check

List Words	Practise	Practise	T	D
leg				
beg				
peg				
hen				
ten				
men				
pen				
den				
they				
no				

Fill the Gaps

1. (a) peg   (b) den   (c) leg

    pe___   de___   le___

    p___ ___   d___ ___   l___ ___

    ___ ___ ___   ___ ___ ___   ___ ___ ___

Word Worm

2. Circle each word you can find in the word worm.

theybegnotenmenpeg

Unit 10

Spelling Sums

3. (a) b + eg = __beg__

   (b) t + en = _____

   (c) l + eg = _____

   (d) h + en = _____

   (e) p + en = _____

What Am I?

4. I am full of ink.

   You use me to write.

   I am a _____.

Spelling Patterns

5. Use the correct colour for these words.

   (a) Colour the 'eg' words blue.

   (b) Colour the 'en' words yellow.

Shape Sorter

6. Guess the word by its shape.

   (a)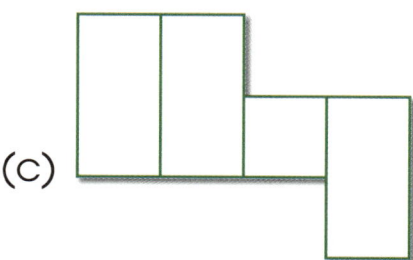

   (b)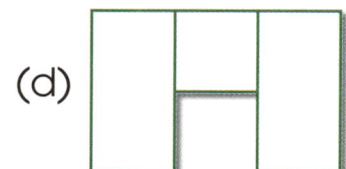

   (c)

   (d)

Unit 10

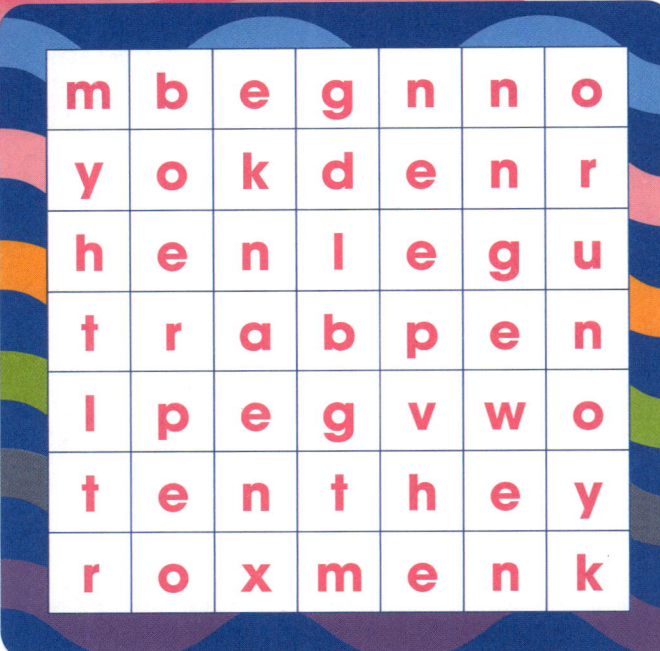

Word Search

7. Find these words in the word search.

leg	men
beg	pen
peg	den
hen	they
ten	no

Word Maker

8. How many words can you make?

_____   _____

_____   _____

_____

List Words

- leg
- beg
- peg
- hen
- ten
- men
- pen
- den
- they
- no

Missing Words

9. Complete the sentences using these words.

(a) He fell and broke his _____.

(b) There were _____ green bottles.

(c) Yesterday, _____ went into town.

(d) The _____ got in the car.

Unit 10

eg en

All Mixed Up

10. Unjumble these words.

(a) ehn _____ (b) yteh _____

(c) gep _____ (d) nde _____

Find Me

11. Circle the correct word.

(a) men

ten

hen

(b) hen

pen

men

(c) peg

egg

leg

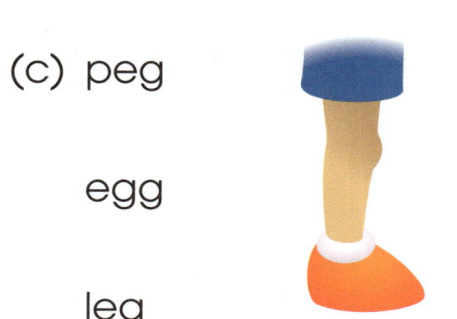

(d) peg

leg

egg

Match Me

12. Circle the word in the box that matches the given word.

(a) they | tey   they   thiy   thay |

(b) peg | peeg   pig   gep   peg |

(c) ten | tan   tem   ten   ton |

Unit 11

List Words	Practise	Practise	T	D
my				
by				
fly				
sky				
mop				
top				
hop				
pop				
for				
on				

Fill the Gaps

1. (a) fly (b) mop (c) sky

   fl___   mo___   sk___

   f___ ___ m___ ___ s___ ___

   ___ ___ ___   ___ ___ ___   ___ ___ ___

Word Hunt

2. Which four words end in '**y**'?

   _____   _____

   _____   _____

Unit 11

Shape Sorter

3. Guess the word by its shape.

(a)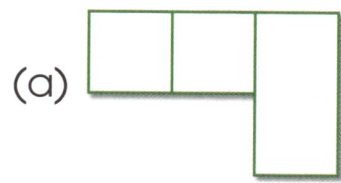

(b)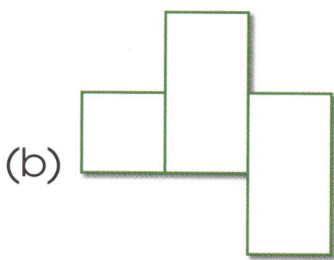

(c)

(d)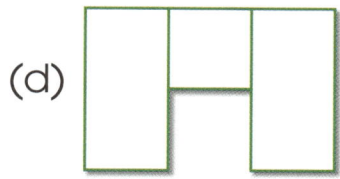

Spelling Sums

4. (a) fl + y = _fly_

   (b) m + op = _____

   (c) h + op = _____

   (d) sk + y = _____

   (e) p + op = _____

What Am I?

5. I am above your head.

   I can be white and blue.

   I am the _____.

Spelling Patterns

6. Use the correct colour for these words.

   (a) Colour the 'y' words orange.

   (b) Colour the 'op' words blue.

Unit 11

k	o	m	o	p	l	s
f	l	y	p	o	r	q
u	y	t	o	p	g	h
l	k	y	e	d	j	o
p	h	l	f	o	r	r
l	o	n	p	l	w	b
a	p	f	e	s	k	y

Word Search

7. Find these words in the word search.

my	top
by	hop
fly	pop
sky	for
mop	on

Word Maker

8. How many words can you make?

_____ _____

_____ _____

h   p

m   t

op

Missing Words

9. Complete the sentences using these words.

   on

(a) I can _____ on one leg.

(b) The cat went to the _____ of the tree.

(c) On a sunny day the _____ is blue.

(d) We walk _____ the shops _____ the way to _____ school.

Word Meanings

10. Match each word to its meaning.

(a) mop — the space above earth

(b) hop — move through the air

(c) fly — jump on one foot

(d) sky — used for washing floors

All Mixed Up

11. Unjumble these words.

(a) orf _____   (b) lyf _____
(c) pom _____   (d) yb _____

Read and Draw

12. A mop and a fly.

List Words: my, by, fly, sky, mop, top, hop, pop, for, on

Unit 12

List Words	Practise	Practise	T	D
see				
been				
weed				
seed				
meet				
need				
feed				
seen				
yes				
saw				

Look
Say
Trace
Cover
Write
Check

Word Worm

1. Circle each word you can find in the word worm.

yesmeetweedsawseebeen

Fill the Gaps

2. (a) weed

wee___

we___ ___

w___ ___ ___

___ ___ ___ ___

(b) seen

see___

se___ ___

s___ ___ ___

___ ___ ___ ___

(c) saw

sa___

s___ ___

___ ___ ___

Unit 12

ee

What Am I?

3. I am small but I can grow tall.

   You can plant me.

   I am a _____.

Shape Sorter

4. Guess the word by its shape.

   (a)

   (b)

   (c)

   (d)

Small Words

5. Write the small words in these big words.

   (a) been   **be**
               bee

   (b) meet   _____

   (c) weed   _____

Spelling Patterns

6. Use the correct colour for these words.

   (a) Colour the 'eed' words red.

   (b) Colour the 'een' words yellow.

feed   **been**   **weed**   **seed**   **seen**   **need**

Unit 12

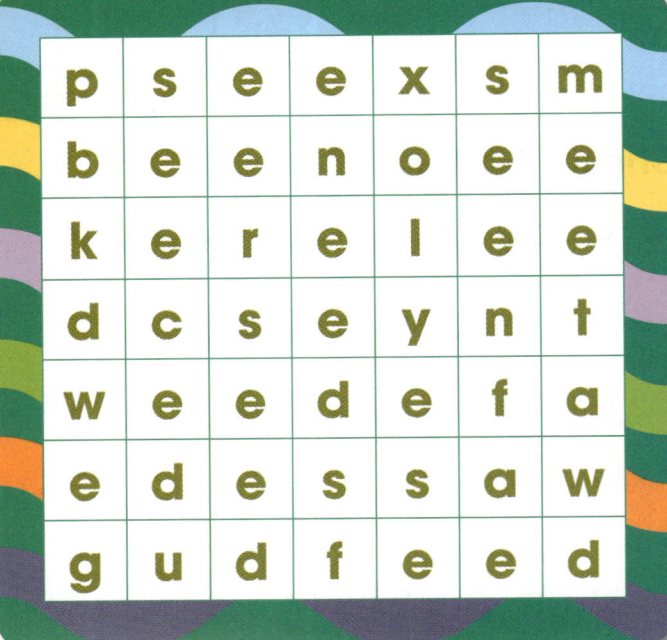

Word Search

7. Find these words in the word search.

see   need

been   feed

weed   seen

seed   yes

meet   saw

Word Maker

8. How many words can you make?

_____   _____

_____   _____

eed

s   f

n   w

Missing Words

9. Complete the sentences using these words.

meet   **been**   **see**   **feed**   **saw**

(a) We all _____ the film.

(b) We will _____ Mum at the shops.

(c) I want to _____ that new film.

(d) We went to _____ bread to the swans.

(e) I have never _____ in her house.

ee

Unit 12

Draw and Label

10. Draw and label

(a) a weed   (b) a seed

All Mixed Up

11. Unjumble these words.

(a) nese _____   (b) wsa _____

(c) teem _____   (d) sey _____

Match Me

12. Circle each word in the bug that matches the given word.

(a) see   cee   sea   see

(b) meet   mete   meet   meat

(c) seed   sead   ceed   seed

List Words

see
been
weed
seed
meet
need
feed
seen
yes
saw

Unit 13

oo | all

List Words	Practise	Practise	T	D
moon				
room				
hood				
zoo				
all				
call				
ball				
small				
this				
have				

Fill the Gaps

1. (a) room   (b) hood   (c) ball

     roo__   hoo__   bal__

     ro__ __   ho__ __   ba__ __

     r__ __ __   h__ __ __   b__ __ __

     __ __ __ __   __ __ __ __   __ __ __ __

More Than One

2. Add 's' to make more than one.

     (a) ball _____   (b) room _____

     (c) moon _____   (d) zoo _____

Unit 13

Spelling Sums

3. (a) m + oon = __moon__

   (b) c + all = _____

   (c) sm + all = _____

   (d) r + oom = _____

   (e) th + is = _____

All Mixed Up

4. Unjumble these words.

   (a) ozo _____

   (b) oorm _____

   (c) aveh _____

   (d) lsalm _____

Shape Sorter

5. Guess the word by its shape.

   (a)

   (b)

   (c)

   (d)

Word Worm

6. Circle each word you can find in the word worm.

Unit 13

Word Search

7. Find these words in the word search.

moon	call
room	ball
hood	small
zoo	this
all	have

What Am I?

8. I keep your head dry.

   I am often on a coat.

   I am a _____.

Missing Words

9. Complete the sentences using these words.

have   ball   zoo   small

(a) I saw a giraffe at the _____.

(b) The _____ rolled down the road.

(c) Ants are very _____.

(d) I _____ a dog called Spot.

List Words: moon, room, hood, zoo, all, call, ball, small, this, have

64   My Spelling Workbook A—Prim-Ed Publishing—www.prim-ed.com

Spelling Patterns

10. (a) Write the 'all' words on the ball.

(b) Write all the other list words in the square.

Missing Letters

11. Write 'oo' or 'all' to make a word.

(a) r_____m (b) sm_____ (c) h_____d

(d) z_____ (e) c_____ (f) m_____n

Secret Words

12. (a) Take the 'm' off 'moon' and put in 's'. _____

(b) Take the 'c' off 'call' and put in 't'. _____

(c) Take the 'h' off 'hood' and put in 'g'. _____

(d) Take the 's' off 'this' and put in 'n'. _____

Unit 14

List Words	Practise	Practise	T	D
and				
sand				
band				
hand				
end				
lend				
send				
bend				
from				
want				

Look, Say, Trace, Cover, Write, Check

Fill the Gaps

1. (a) band   (b) want   (c) send

    ban___   wan___   sen___

    ba___ ___   wa___ ___   se___ ___

    b___ ___ ___   w___ ___ ___   s___ ___ ___

    ___ ___ ___ ___   ___ ___ ___ ___   ___ ___ ___ ___

Word Hunt

2. (a) Which word has a small insect in it? _____

   (b) Which word can you find on a beach? _____

   (c) Write the two smallest words. _____ _____

   (d) Which two words start with 'b'? _____ _____

Unit 14

What Am I?

3. I am part of your body.

You have two of me.

I can do lots of things.

I am a _____.

Spelling Sums

4. (a) w + ant = _____

(b) s + and = _____

(c) h + and = _____

(d) b + end = _____

(e) fr + om = _____

All Mixed Up

5. Unjumble these words.

(a) dne   _____

(b) dnah   _____

(c) dna   _____

(d) dnes   _____

Match Me

6. Circle the word in the ball that matches the given word.

(a) from

(b) band

(c) lend

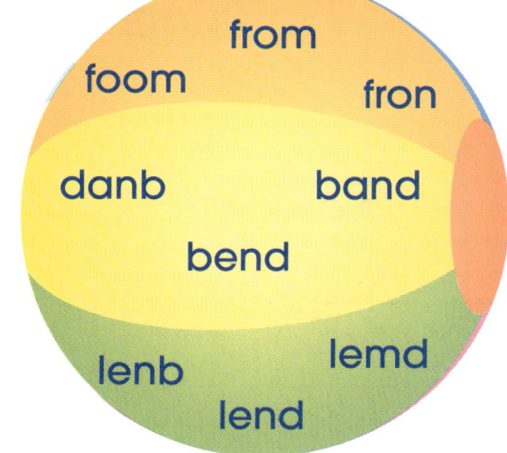

Unit 14

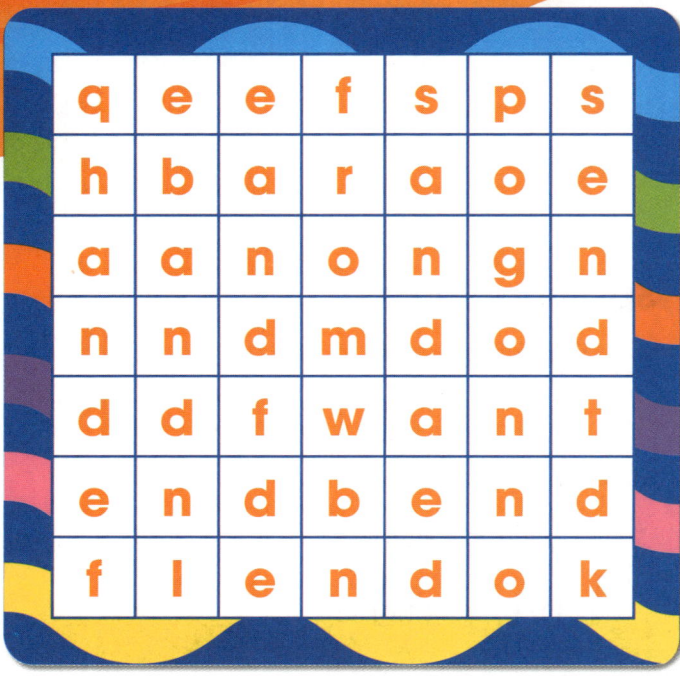

Word Search

7. Find these words in the word search.

and	end
sand	send
band	bend
hand	from
lend	want

Missing Letters

8. (a) ___r___m (b) l___ ___d (c) h___n___

   (d) be___ ___ (e) ___ ___nt (f) a___ ___

Missing Words

9. Complete the sentences using these words.

sand   send   from   and

(a) She likes to eat fish _____ chips.

(b) Can you _____ me a letter?

(c) It is a long way _____ school to my house.

(d) Can you feel the hot _____ on the beach with your toes?

List Words

and
sand
band
hand
end
lend
send
bend
from
want

Read and Draw

10. A girl with a blue band in her hair playing in the sandpit.

Secret Words

11. (a) Take the 'm' off 'from' and put in 'st'. _____

(b) Take the 'nt' off 'want' and put in 'sp'. _____

(c) Take the 'd' off 'send' and put in 't'. _____

(d) Take the 'h' off 'hand' and put in 'l'. _____

Spelling Patterns

12. Use the correct colour for these words.

(a) Colour all the 'and' words red.

(b) Colour all the 'end' words green.

(c) Colour all the other words blue.

bend   **from**

band

end

want   **hand**

Unit 15 — Summer Holidays

List Words	Practise	Practise	T	D
cap				
map				
car				
hat				
fun				
run				
ball				
net				
also				
one				

Look · Say · Trace · Cover · Write · Check

Rhyming Words

1. Write a summer word that rhymes with these words.

   (a) far _____   (b) hall _____

   (c) sun _____   (d) vet _____

   (e) rat _____   (f) rap _____

Word Worm

2. Circle each word you can find in the word worm.

oneballalsohatcapfun

70 My Spelling Workbook A—Prim-Ed Publishing—www.prim-ed.com

Summer Holidays

Unit 15

All Mixed Up

3. Unjumble these words.

   (a) noe _____

   (b) labl _____

   (c) laso _____

   (d) tne _____

Shape Sorter

4. Guess the word by its shape.

   (a)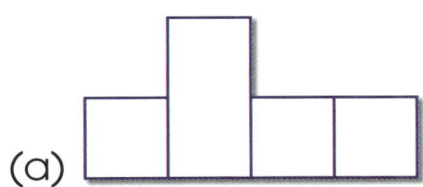

   (b)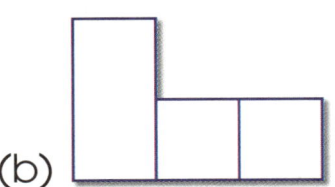

   (c)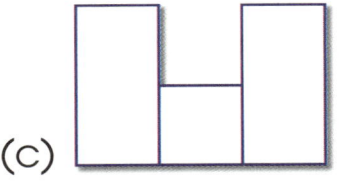

   (d)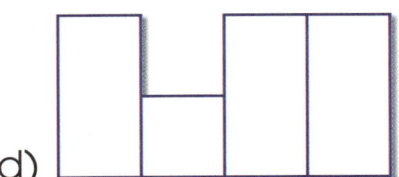

Read and Draw

5. A ball going into a net.

Find the Word

6. Write each word on the grid.

   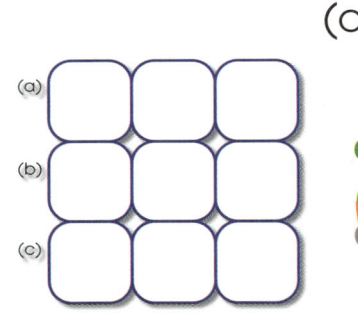

   (a)

   (b)

   (c)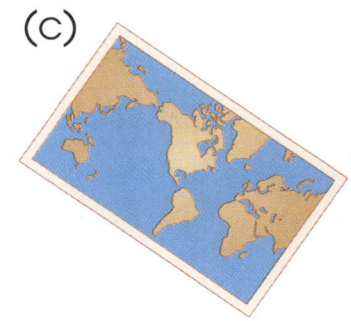

Summer Holidays

Word Search

7. Find these words in the sunshine word search.

cap   run
map   ball
car   net
hat   also
fun   one

Word Maker

8. How many list words can you make from the letters on the beach ball?

_____ _____ _____

List Words

cap
map
car
hat
fun
run
ball
net
also
one

Missing Words

9. Complete the sentences using these words.

(a) Dad drives his _____ too fast.

(b) Use the _____ to find the way.

(c) Add _____ to two to get three.

(d) Put a _____ on when in the sun.

Summer Holidays

Unit 15

Labels

10. Label the pictures.

(a)

_____

(b)

_____

(c)

_____

(d)

_____

Word Hunt

11. (a) Which words end with '**un**'? _____ _____

(b) Which words have four letters? _____ _____

(c) Which word has the small word '**at**' in it? _____

Fill the Gaps

12. (a) also

als___

al___ ___

a___ ___ ___

___ ___ ___ ___

(b) run

ru___

r___ ___

___ ___ ___

(c) one

on___

o___ ___

___ ___ ___

Difficult Words I Have Found

Word	Practise	Practise	Practise

My Spelling Dictionary Aa to Ff

Aa

Bb

Cc

Dd

Ee

Ff

My Spelling Dictionary Gg to Ll

Gg

Hh

Ii

Jj

Kk

Ll

My Spelling Dictionary Mm to Ss

Mm

Nn

Oo

Pp

Qq

Rr

Ss

My Spelling Dictionary Tt to Zz

Tt

Uu

Vv

Ww

Xx

Yy

Zz